IT'S SCIENCE!

Time

IT'S SCIENCE!

Time

Sally Hewitt

CHILDREN'S PRESS®

A Division of Grolier Publishing

NEW YORK • LONDON • HONG KONG • SYDNEY
DANBURY, CONNECTICUT

Acknowledgments:
Antique Clocks Gerard Campbell p. 13r; Eye Ubiquitous p. 15bl (Sean Aidan);
Frank Lane Picture Agency p. 25l (John Karmali); Image Bank p. 26tr;
Images Colour Library pp. 22, 23tl; Oxford Scientific Films pp. 20 (Richard Packwood),
23c (Owen Newman), 25tr (Martyn Colbeck); Planet Earth Pictures p. 23bl (Allan Parker);
The Stock Market p. 27c; Tony Stone Images pp. 23tr (Gary Vesta), 25br (Laurence Monneret),
27t (Alistair Beck). Thanks, too, to our models: Luke Jackson-Abeson, Nading Gupta,
Thomas James and Fay Beaman.

Series editor: Rachel Cooke
Designer: Mo Choy
Consultant: Sally Nankivell-Aston
Photography: Ray Moller unless otherwise acknowledged
Picture research: Sue Mennell

First published in 1999 by Franklin Watts
96 Leonard Street, London EC2A 4RH

First American edition 1999 by Children's Press
A division of Grolier Publishing
90 Sherman Turnpike
Danbury, CT 06816

Visit Franklin Watts on the Internet at:
http://publishing.grolier.com

ISBN 0-516-21655-4
A CIP catalog record for this book is
available from the Library of Congress

Contents

What's the Time?

Do you sometimes ask the question "What's the time?"

Do you know what time you go to school in the morning?

What time do you have lunch?

What is your bedtime?

Do you go to school, have lunch, and go to bed at the same time every day?

💡 THINK ABOUT IT!

What would happen if you went to school at any time you chose — not at the right time? Would your friends and teachers be there at the same time as you?

6

Knowing how to tell the time helps you to be "on time."

What happens when you are early?

What happens when you are on time?

What happens when you are too late?

TRY IT OUT!

Make a list like this one of some of the things you will do tomorrow.

Can you write the time you should be doing each one? Will it matter if you are late for any of these things?

Wake up - 7 o'clock
Breakfast - 8 o'clock
School - 9 o'clock
Lunch - 12.30
Football - 4 o'clock
TV program - 5.30
Supper - 6 o'clock
Bedtime - 8 o'clock

Time Passing

You can't see time, but it is always moving on. How much time passes while Adam makes his model?

It takes Adam an **hour** to finish the helicopter. Some of the things you do only take **minutes** or even **seconds**.

TRY IT OUT!

Guess how long it takes you to comb your hair, brush your teeth, or get dressed. Check your watch to see how long you actually take to do these things. Were you right?

Your hair is growing all the time but very slowly so you can't see it happening. It takes about 6 **weeks** for your hair to grow about 3/4 in (2 cm).

After you have been to the hairdresser, how long do you wait before it is time to get your hair cut again?

A whole **year** passes between birthdays.

 **TRY IT OUT!**

Do you have photographs of yourself on two birthdays in a row — perhaps your last birthday and the one before? Can you see how much you have changed and grown in the time it has taken for one year to pass? Can you still fit into clothes you wore a year ago?

9

Day and Night

We see time moving on as day becomes night and night becomes day.

12 o'clock in the middle of the day is called midday or noon.

Daytime begins when the sun rises in the morning.

Afternoon is the part of the day that comes after noon.

Evening is at the end of the afternoon. The sun sets and it becomes dark.

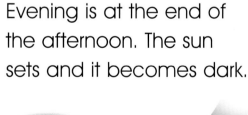

THINK ABOUT IT!

What do you do at these different times of day?

12 o'clock in the middle of the night is called midnight.

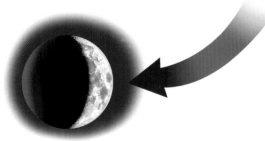

10

Day and night happen because Earth, the planet we live on, is round and is spinning in space. It looks to us as though the sun is moving across the sky, but we are actually moving as Earth spins around.

It takes 24 hours — one whole **day** — for Earth to spin all the way around once. The part of Earth facing the sun changes as it spins.

It is daytime when the part of Earth you are on is facing the sun.

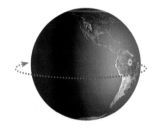

It is nighttime when the part you are on is facing away from the sun.

 TRY IT OUT!

On a sunny day early in the morning, push a stick into soft ground. Mark where the shadow falls. Keep marking the shadow of the stick at different times of the day. What do you notice?

Measuring Time

Do you have a watch? Is there a clock on your kitchen wall? We use clocks and watches to measure time. In the past, people used candles, sand, and water to measure time.

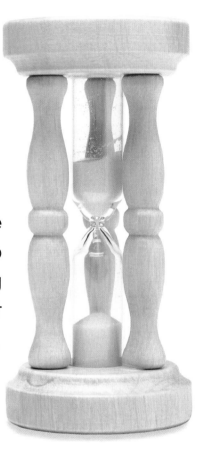

It takes an hour for the wax to burn down from one mark to the next on this candle.

It takes 5 minutes for the sand to flow from the top to the bottom of this egg timer — just the time it takes to boil an egg.

 TRY IT OUT!

People used to measure time with a bowl that took a certain amount of time to sink. You can make a simple time measurer, too. Shape a shallow bowl out of aluminum foil. Use a pencil point to push a small hole in the bottom. Put it in water and time how long it takes to sink.

Watches and clocks have different ways of keeping time that are much more accurate.

A small **spring** inside this watch gradually uncurls to make the hands move around.

A **pendulum** swinging steadily backward and forward keeps some clocks ticking.

Inside this watch is a battery with a piece of **quartz crystal** that is always moving back and forth a tiny bit. Each move back and forth always takes exactly the same amount of time. Quartz watches keep very accurate time.

 LOOK AGAIN

Look again at page 7. Why do we need to measure passing time? Look again at page 11 to find another way to measure time.

Counting the Hours

Clocks and watches measure time in hours, minutes, and seconds. There are 60 minutes in an hour and 60 seconds in a minute.

It takes about one second to clap your hands once.

It takes about one minute to build a tower this high.

It takes about an hour to bake a potato in an oven.

 LOOK AGAIN

Look again at page 11 to find out how many hours there are in a day.

14

The big hand on this clock face moves around to show the passing minutes.
The small hand moves much more slowly and shows the passing hours.

On a digital clock, the numbers on the left of the two dots show the hours. The numbers on the right of the two dots show the minutes.

A stopwatch can measure even smaller amounts of time than a second. Runners are often timed with a stopwatch. Sometimes less than a second decides who is the winner of a race.

THINK ABOUT IT!

What do you think you can do in an hour? What can you do that only takes a minute? What can you do in just one second?

What's the Date?

A year is divided into **months**, weeks, and days. You can check the date and find facts about a year in a **diary** or a **calendar** like this.

YEAR 2000

JANUARY
Sun	Mon	Tues	Wed	Thur	Fri	Sat
						1
2	3	4	5	6	7	8
9	10	11	12	13	14	15
16	17	18	19	20	21	22
23	24	25	26	27	28	29
30	31					

FEBRUARY
Sun	Mon	Tues	Wed	Thur	Fri	Sat
		1	2	3	4	5
6	7	8	9	10	11	12
13	14	15	16	17	18	19
20	21	22	23	24	25	26
27	28	29				

MARCH
Sun	Mon	Tues	Wed	Thur	Fri	Sat
			1	2	3	4
5	6	7	8	9	10	11
12	13	14	15	16	17	18
19	20	21	22	23	24	25
26	27	28	29	30	31	

APRIL
Sun	Mon	Tues	Wed	Thur	Fri	Sat
						1
2	3	4	5	6	7	8
9	10	11	12	13	14	15
16	17	18	19	20	21	22
23	24	25	26	27	28	29
30						

MAY
Sun	Mon	Tues	Wed	Thur	Fri	Sat
	1	2	3	4	5	6
7	8	9	10	11	12	13
14	15	16	17	18	19	20
21	22	23	24	25	26	27
28	29	30	31			

JUNE
Sun	Mon	Tues	Wed	Thur	Fri	Sat
				1	2	3
4	5	6	7	8	9	10
11	12	13	14	15	16	17
18	19	20	21	22	23	24
25	26	27	28	29	30	

JULY
Sun	Mon	Tues	Wed	Thur	Fri	Sat
						1
2	3	4	5	6	7	8
9	10	11	12	13	14	15
16	17	18	19	20	21	22
23	24	25	26	27	28	29
30	31					

AUGUST
Sun	Mon	Tues	Wed	Thur	Fri	Sat
		1	2	3	4	5
6	7	8	9	10	11	12
13	14	15	16	17	18	19
20	21	22	23	24	25	26
27	28	29	30	31		

SEPTEMBER
Sun	Mon	Tues	Wed	Thur	Fri	Sat
					1	2
3	4	5	6	7	8	9
10	11	12	13	14	15	16
17	18	19	20	21	22	23
24	25	26	27	28	29	30

OCTOBER
Sun	Mon	Tues	Wed	Thur	Fri	Sat
1	2	3	4	5	6	7
8	9	10	11	12	13	14
15	16	17	18	19	20	21
22	23	24	25	26	27	28
29	30	31				

NOVEMBER
Sun	Mon	Tues	Wed	Thur	Fri	Sat
			1	2	3	4
5	6	7	8	9	10	11
12	13	14	15	16	17	18
19	20	21	22	23	24	25
26	27	28	29	30		

DECEMBER
Sun	Mon	Tues	Wed	Thur	Fri	Sat
					1	2
3	4	5	6	7	8	9
10	11	12	13	14	15	16
17	18	19	20	21	22	23
24	25	26	27	28	29	30
31						

TRY IT OUT!

Use the calendar to check out these facts about a year.

How many months are there in a year?

There are 365 days in a year. Every four years there is a leap year — it has one extra day, which makes 366 days. The extra day is in February, which is usually only 28 days long. Is 2000 a leap year?

Can you find your birthday on the calendar?

There are 7 days in a week. How many weeks are there in a year?

We often write the date like this: 8/7/00

This number shows the month.

This shows the day.

This number shows the year.

8/7/00

Can you find this date on the calendar?

A diary can help you plan ahead and remember important dates. It can help you remember the things you have done, too.

A Year

Earth does not just spin. It also moves in an enormous loop around the sun. It takes a whole year for Earth to go all the way around once.

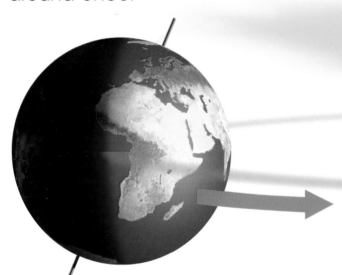

Earth is tilted so that the half nearer to the sun is warmer than the half farther from the sun.

👁 LOOK AGAIN

Look again at page 11 to find out how long it takes for Earth to spin around once. Look again at page 16 to figure out how many times it spins around in one year.

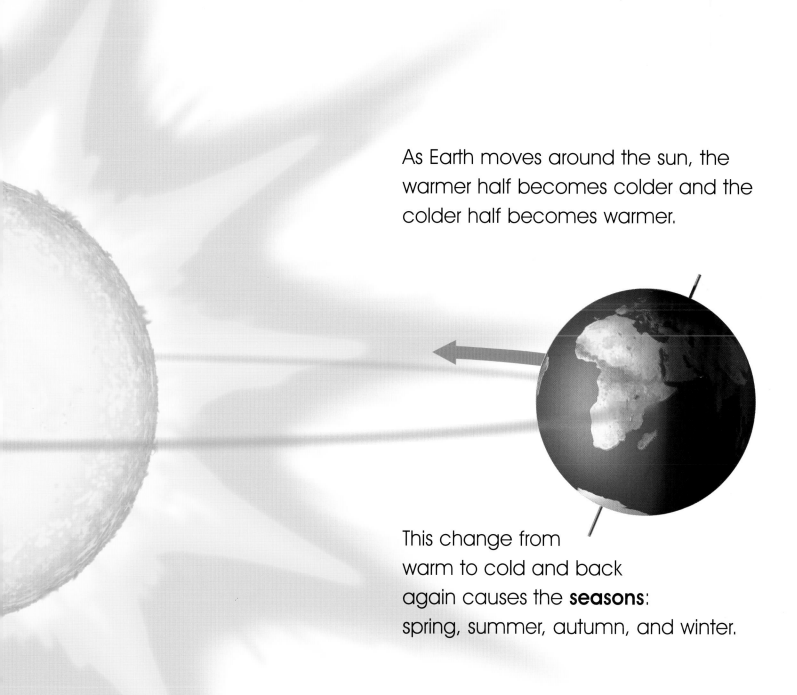

As Earth moves around the sun, the warmer half becomes colder and the colder half becomes warmer.

This change from warm to cold and back again causes the **seasons**: spring, summer, autumn, and winter.

💡 **THINK ABOUT IT!**

What is the weather like at the moment? Do you think the part of Earth where you live is tilting toward the sun or away from it at the moment?

Seasons

The seasons change from spring, to summer, autumn, winter, and then back to spring again. Each season brings different kinds of weather. Follow the arrows to see how the seasons follow each other during the year.

When spring comes, the weather starts to get warm after the cold winter.

Winter is the coldest season. Sometimes snow falls and you have to wear your warmest clothes outside.

In the autumn it starts to get colder again. Leaves on some trees begin to change color and fall to the ground.

Summer brings hot weather. It is a good time to play outside.

 TRY IT OUT!

Make a seasons wheel.
You need two paper plates and a
paper fastener. With a pen, divide
each plate into quarters.

In the quarters of one plate,
draw a picture of each
season. Cut one quarter
out of the other plate,
leaving a section at its
center to push the paper
fastener through.

Put this plate on top of the other
plate and fix them together at the
center with the paper fastener.

Move the top plate around
to show each season
in turn.

Natural Clocks

Plants and animals do not have clocks or watches like we do.

They tell the time by sensing natural changes such as the weather getting colder or the days getting shorter.

These changes are like natural clocks that help them know when to grow or when it is time to get ready for the cold winter ahead.

👁 LOOK AGAIN

Look again at page 10 to find something that happens naturally to wake you in the morning.

Spring is a good time for birds to lay eggs because the chicks will hatch in the summer when there is plenty of food around.

Flowers bloom in the warm summer sun. This is the time when there are plenty of insects around to visit them and carry **pollen** from flower to flower.

Flocks of swallows gather together at the end of summer. They know that soon there will not be enough to eat, so they will make a very long journey to find food.

Autumn is the time that dormice fatten themselves up while there is still plenty of food.

They sleep all winter, using up the food they have stored as fat in their bodies.

 LOOK AGAIN

Look again at page 20 to find what some trees do when the weather begins to get cold in the autumn.

Always Changing

How long can you stand still? Time never stands still; it is always moving on. Even if you stand still all day, things around you change.

People, animals, and plants are always changing and growing.

 **TRY IT OUT!**

Plant some seeds in dirt and put the pots in a warm, sunny place. Water them and look for the first signs of shoots. Watch the plants change and grow a little bit every day.

 LOOK AGAIN

Look again at page 9 to find something that is always growing on your head.

Different creatures take different amounts of time to grow. Some are born tiny and helpless; others can look after themselves right away.

This baby elephant will stay with its mother until it is 10 years old, and it will not stop growing until it is about 25!

A baby bird can look after itself only a few weeks after hatching!

You will be fully grown when you are about 20 years old. But your body will still keep changing.

 THINK ABOUT IT!

How do you think you will continue to change as you grow older? What do you think you will look like when you are 20 years old? What do you think you will look like when you are 50?

Fast and Slow

Everyone knows that a hare can run very quickly and that a tortoise lumbers slowly along. As long as the hare does not stop for a nap, it will easily win a race against a tortoise!

The winner of a race is the one who gets to the finishing line first. They are the fastest — they have taken the smallest amount of time to run the race.

 TRY IT OUT!

How fast can you write your name, put on your shoes and socks, or deal a pack of cards into two equal piles? To find out, get a friend to time you using the second hand on a watch or clock, or use a stopwatch if you have one. Try the tasks again. Can you do them faster?

 THINK ABOUT IT!

Is it always a good idea to do something very fast? Can you think of anything that you should do slowly?

It takes a passenger liner about 5 days to sail across the Atlantic Ocean from England to America.

It can take the Concorde less than 3 hours to fly across the Atlantic Ocean from London to New York.

We often need to measure how fast something is going — its **speed**. A **speedometer** measures the speed of a car in miles or kilometers per hour. If a car's speed is 31 miles per hour (50 kilometers per hour), it will travel 31 miles (50 kilometers) in one hour.

Signs on the roads tell drivers how fast they are allowed to go. Drivers have to check their speedometers to make sure they aren't going too fast.

Useful Words

Calendar A calendar lists the months, weeks, and days of a year. It shows on which day of the week a particular date falls.

Day A day is the time it takes for Earth to spin around once. It is 24 hours long. Sometimes, we use the word "day" to describe the time when it is light, between sunrise and sunset.

Diary A diary is a book that is divided into days, weeks, and months. In it, you write dates to remember or things that have happened.

Hour A day is divided into 24 hours. It takes 1 hour for the big hand on a clock to go all the way around. There are 60 minutes in an hour.

Minute An hour is divided into 60 minutes. If you count to 60, saying your name between each number, about a minute will have passed. There are 60 seconds in a minute.

Month A year is divided into 12 months. Most months are 31 days long, except April, June, September, and November, which have 30 days, and February, which usually has 28. In a leap year, February is 29 days long.

Pendulum A pendulum is a hanging weight that swings backward and forward at a constant speed. Some clocks use pendulums to keep time.

Pollen Pollen is the yellow dust in flowers that plants use to make seeds. Pollen has to be moved from one flower to another to form a seed.

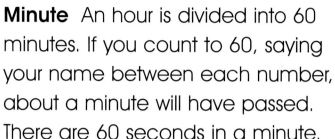

Quartz crystal Quartz crystal is a type of rock. A tiny piece of crystal is used inside the batteries of some watches and clocks to keep time.

Season On certain parts of Earth, the seasons change through a year from spring to summer, autumn, and winter. Each season has different weather that affects plants and animals.

Second A second is a small amount of time, about the length of a hand clap. There are 60 seconds in a minute.

Speed Speed is how fast something is going. Fast and slow are words we use to describe speed. We measure speed by seeing how long it takes something to move a certain distance.

Speedometer A speedometer is an instrument for measuring speed.

Spring A spring is a piece of wire that has been coiled around and around. If it is squashed or stretched, it will try to push or pull itself back into shape. "Spring" is also the name we give to the season after winter, when the weather starts to become warmer.

Week There are 7 days in a week: Monday, Tuesday, Wednesday, Thursday, Friday, Saturday, and Sunday. We call Saturday and Sunday the weekend.

Year A year is how long it takes for Earth to move all the way around the sun. There are 12 months and 365 days in a year. Every fourth year is a leap year, when there are 366 days.

Index

About This Book

Children are natural scientists. They learn by touching and feeling, noticing, asking questions, and trying things out for themselves. The books in the *It's Science!* series are designed for the way children learn. Familiar objects are used as starting points for further learning. *Time* starts by asking "What's the time?" and explores the ways we measure time and see time passing.

Each double-page spread introduces a new topic, such as natural clocks. Information is given, questions asked, and activities suggested that encourage children to make discoveries and develop new ideas for themselves. Look for these panels throughout the book:

TRY IT OUT! indicates a simple activity, using safe materials, that proves or explores a point.
THINK ABOUT IT! indicates a question inspired by the information on the page but that points the reader to areas not covered by the book.
LOOK AGAIN introduces a cross-referencing activity that links themes and facts through the book.

Encourage children not to take the familiar world for granted. Point things out, ask questions, and enjoy making scientific discoveries together.